STUDY GUIDE

INDISPENSABLE
CHURCH

Powerful Ways to Flood Your
Community with Love

ISBN: 978-1-960678-45-4   1 2 3 4 5 6 7 8 9 10

Printed in the United States of America

STUDY GUIDE

CHRIS SONKSEN

INDISPENSABLE
CHURCH

Powerful Ways to Flood Your
Community with Love

ARROWS &
STONES

CONTENTS

CAN YOU IMAGINE . . . ?

Can you imagine how many people would want to come to your church if they were loved simply for who they are?

READING TIME

As you read Chapter 1: "Can You Imagine . . . ?" in *Indispensable Church*, review, reflect on, and respond to the text by answering the following questions.

REFLECT AND TAKE ACTION:

Do you feel your church does a good job of showing love? What would you rate your church on a scale of 1-10?

1   2   3   4   5   6   7   8   9   10

_____

_____

_____

_____

_____

_____

_____

_____

_____

Is your church currently involved in your community? If so, list a couple of ways it makes an impact.

_____

_____

_____

_____

_____

_____

_____

_____

_____

If your church disappeared overnight, would anyone in your community notice? Who? Why?

_____

_____

_____

_____

_____

_____

_____

_____

_____

How much time did Jesus spend with insiders, and how much time did He spend in the lives of those in the communities to which He traveled? What can we learn through His example?

_____

_____

_____

_____

_____

_____

_____

_____

_____

What are you hoping to gain from this book? What aspect of your church do you feel needs the most work?

_____

_____

_____

_____

_____

_____

_____

_____

_____

What do you imagine moving forward for your church? Increased influence? More community outreach?

_____

_____

_____

_____

_____

_____

_____

_____

_____

LOVE IS A VERB

What's the nature of love? It's sacrificial. It gives until it hurts, and it gives some more.

READING TIME

As you read Chapter 2: "Love Is a Verb" in *Indispensable Church*, review, reflect on, and respond to the text by answering the following questions.

REFLECT AND TAKE ACTION:

In your own words, why is it important to recognize love as a verb?

_____

_____

_____

_____

_____

_____

_____

How can we come to love others unconditionally? Is this even possible?

_____

_____

_____

_____

_____

_____

What stands out to you from Jack's story in the opening of this chapter? What actions led to Jack's heart change?

_____

_____

_____

_____

_____

_____

> *Whoever does not love does not know God, because God is love. This is how God showed his love among us: He sent his one and only Son into the world that we might live through him. This is love: not that we loved God, but that he loved us and sent his Son as an atoning sacrifice for our sins.*
>
> *—1 John 4:8–10*

Consider the scripture above and answer the following questions:

What does this verse reveal to us about God's love?

_____

_____

_____

_____

_____

How can we model our love for others after God's love for us?

_____

_____

_____

_____

_____

Have you ever had a misconception about God or His love for you? What was it? How did you clear this misconception up?

_____

_____

_____

_____

_____

Is it true that "compassion inevitably produces loving action"? Why or why not?

_____

_____

_____

_____

_____

Why is it important for new believers to get involved in loving others early in their walk? What is the danger if this does not take place?

_____

_____

_____

_____

_____

How did the Pharisees' "love" differ from that of Jesus?

_____

_____

_____

_____

_____

Who in your life can you more intentionally show love and gratitude for? List as many as you can think of.

_____

_____

_____

_____

_____

MY NEIGHBOR

Loving our neighbor as ourselves doesn't have racial, social, or economic limits.

READING TIME

As you read Chapter 3: "My Neighbor" in *Indispensable Church*, review, reflect on, and respond to the text by answering the following questions.

REFLECT AND TAKE ACTION:

What can we learn from the story of the Good Samaritan, told by Jesus?

_____

_____

_____

_____

_____

_____

_____

_____

_____

Has past violence, silence, ignorance, or absence affected your ability to love others? Share how you believe your situation affected you.

_____

_____

_____

_____

_____

_____

_____

_____

_____

_____

> On one occasion an expert in the law stood
> up to test Jesus. "Teacher," he asked, "what
> must I do to inherit eternal life?"
>
> "What is written in the Law?" he
> replied. "How do you read it?"
>
> He answered, "'Love the Lord your God with all your heart
> and with all your soul and with all your strength and with
> all your mind; and, 'Love your neighbor as yourself.'"
>
> "You have answered correctly," Jesus
> replied. "Do this and you will live."
>
> —Luke 10:25-28

Consider the scripture above and answer the following questions:

Do you find it harder to love God or love others? Why?

_____

_____

_____

_____

_____

_____

_____

_____

Is this really all it takes to inherit eternal life? Why or why not?

_____

_____

_____

_____

_____

_____

_____

_____

How do the values of God's kingdom differ from the values of the world?

_____

_____

_____

_____

_____

_____

_____

_____

_____

Which of the three "walls" that people place (race, social status, politics) do you think is most prevalent in today's society? Have you ever been guilty of putting one (or more) of these walls up?

_____

_____

_____

_____

_____

_____

_____

_____

_____

In what three ways do acts of kindness add value to the lives of recipients? Did any of these surprise you?

_____

_____

_____

_____

_____

_____

_____

_____

_____

_____

_____

Whose life can you add value to today? Write down which neighbor you want to bless, how you want to do it, and a practical timetable for making it happen.

_____

_____

_____

_____

_____

_____

_____

_____

_____

_____

_____

WHY IS IT SO HARD?

Love changes everything, but we don't just wake up one morning and love like Jesus.

READING TIME

As you read Chapter 4: "Why Is It So Hard?" in *Indispensable Church*, review, reflect on, and respond to the text by answering the following questions.

REFLECT AND TAKE ACTION:

Have you ever found it difficult to love someone? If so, why? Was it something they had done in the past? Something about their current life you didn't agree with?

_____

_____

_____

_____

_____

_____

Why is attempting to live well enough to be accepted by God counterproductive? What is the error in this way of thinking?

_____

_____

_____

_____

_____

_____

How are wonder and our ability to love others tied together?

_____

_____

_____

_____

_____

_____

How does God's love change our lives?

_____

_____

_____

_____

_____

_____

_____

_____

_____

What are some of the prerequisites to loving like Jesus did?

_____

_____

_____

_____

_____

_____

_____

_____

_____

How does your certainty about your ultimate hope give you courage to love, care for, and show grace to others?

_____

_____

_____

_____

_____

_____

_____

_____

How do outsiders view your church when it comes to the impact it is making on the community?

_____

_____

_____

_____

_____

_____

_____

_____

Take time to introspect and uproot anything that is inhibiting your relationship with God or your love for others.

THE CALL

We don't stumble into our purpose;
God awakens us into it.

READING TIME

As you read Chapter 5: "The Call" in *Indispensable Church*, review, reflect on, and respond to the text by answering the following questions.

REFLECT AND TAKE ACTION:

What do you feel God has called you to do?

_____

_____

_____

_____

_____

_____

Does God reveal His full calling and plans to us up front? Why do you think this is?

_____

_____

_____

_____

_____

_____

Why is it important for us to recognize we are collaborators with Christ and not co-stars?

_____

_____

_____

_____

_____

_____

_____

> *Therefore, I urge you, brothers and sisters, in view of God's mercy, to offer your bodies as a living sacrifice, holy and pleasing to God—this is your true and proper worship. Do not conform to the pattern of this world, but be transformed by the renewing of your mind. Then you will be able to test and approve what God's will is—his good, pleasing and perfect will.*
>
> *—Romans 12:1-2*

Consider the scripture above and answer the following questions:

What does it mean to offer one's body as a "living and holy sacrifice"?

_____

_____

_____

_____

_____

_____

_____

_____

Do you think offering our bodies as a sacrifice is a one-time decision or an ongoing process? Explain your answer.

_____

_____

_____

_____

_____

_____

_____

Does being "called by God" mean that you're called to preach and/or serve in a church? Why or why not?

_____

_____

_____

_____

_____

_____

What stands out to you about Abraham's call from God? How can you apply this to your own calling?

_____

_____

_____

_____

_____

_____

How does the Holy Spirit help us understand God's calling? Does His help stop here?

_____

_____

_____

_____

_____

_____

_____

START SMALL . . . BUT START!

God doesn't give us the chair; He gives us the wood and the skill we need to make it.

READING TIME

As you read Chapter 6: "Start Small . . . but Start!" in *Indispensable Church*, review, reflect on, and respond to the text by answering the following questions.

REFLECT AND TAKE ACTION:

How do you think the boy whose lunch was multiplied by Jesus felt after the miracle took place?

_____
_____
_____
_____
_____
_____
_____
_____
_____
_____

Did the boy have any part in this miracle? If so, what? What can we learn from his involvement?

_____
_____
_____
_____
_____
_____
_____
_____
_____
_____
_____

In your own words, what does it mean that "miracles follow actions"?

_____

_____

_____

_____

_____

_____

_____

_____

_____

_____

Why is our love for one another so important to Jesus that He continuously repeats it throughout His ministry?

_____

_____

_____

_____

_____

_____

_____

_____

_____

_____

When someone lashes out at you or wrongs you, how do you respond? How can looking at it in a different light affect your response?

_____

_____

_____

_____

_____

_____

_____

_____

What is the first step for you? Take time to write out your first step in detail, no matter how small it may be.

_____

_____

_____

_____

_____

_____

_____

_____

_____

MAKE IT HAPPEN

When churches mobilize their people to get involved in meeting the needs of the community, amazing things happen.

READING TIME

As you read Chapter 7: "Make It Happen" in *Indispensable Church*, review, reflect on, and respond to the text by answering the following questions.

REFLECT AND TAKE ACTION:

How will you select the leaders of your Love Where You Live effort? Why are administratively-gifted individuals important to choose for this task?

_____

_____

_____

_____

_____

_____

_____

_____

_____

Brainstorm some people that would be great on the Love Where You Live team. Who are they? Why would they be positive additions to the team?

_____

_____

_____

_____

_____

_____

_____

_____

_____

_____

What are some organizations you can consider supporting/
partnering with for your first (or next) Love Where You Live
event?

_____

_____

_____

_____

_____

_____

_____

_____

_____

What are some possible activities your church can perform for
your next Love Where You Live event?

_____

_____

_____

_____

_____

_____

_____

_____

_____

How many Love Where You Live events do you feel your church could focus on and execute effectively?

_____

_____

_____

_____

_____

_____

_____

_____

_____

Take time to pick a potential leader, team, and organization/ activity, then create a rough plan for your next Love Where You Live event.

_____

_____

_____

_____

_____

_____

_____

_____

_____

_____

WOVEN INTO THE FABRIC

Jesus taught people about grace, forgiveness, and the kingdom of God, but always in the context of connecting and caring.

READING TIME

As you read Chapter 8: "Woven Into the Fabric" in *Indispensable Church*, review, reflect on, and respond to the text by answering the following questions.

REFLECT AND TAKE ACTION:

What parts of the community is your church already connected with? What parts of the community would you like your church to get more involved in?

_____

_____

_____

_____

_____

What community leaders, if any, do you know personally? How do they tend to view churches in the area?

_____

_____

_____

_____

_____

If your church hasn't had a Love Where You Live Saturday yet, how would you prioritize your list of the nonprofits and agencies as possible partners for the event?

_____

_____

_____

_____

_____

_____

If your church has had at least one event, which additional community and nonprofit leaders do you think would make good partners? How can you build relationships with these leaders without them thinking they're no more than a project to you?

_____

_____

_____

_____

_____

_____

_____

_____

How will the above help to weave you and your church into the fabric of the community?

_____

_____

_____

_____

_____

_____

_____

_____

_____

How do you stay connected and current with people? How could your system improve?

_____

_____

_____

_____

_____

_____

_____

_____

_____

Can you tell when someone loves the people you love? How does this make you feel?

_____

_____

_____

_____

_____

_____

_____

_____

_____

CHAPTER 9

CREATE A MOVEMENT

Movements are like rivers. A bucket of water doesn't have much of an impact on geography, but even a relatively slow river carves the landscape, breaking down banks, depositing sediments, and changing its course. Momentum has a powerful impact.

REFLECT AND TAKE ACTION:

What movement(s) have you been a part of? What was its purpose? How did it make you feel?

_____

_____

_____

_____

_____

_____

How do the principles of the rock and the flywheel apply to you and your efforts to implement Love Where You Live?

_____

_____

_____

_____

_____

_____

What practical steps could you take to make selflessly serving others a normal occurrence in your church?

_____

_____

_____

_____

_____

_____

What difference do you think it would make if serving others became a norm within your church?

_____

_____

_____

_____

_____

_____

_____

_____

_____

Which of the stages of growth is your church currently in? What steps do you need to take for your church to advance to the next stage?

_____

_____

_____

_____

_____

_____

_____

_____

_____

_____

Which of the benefits in the last section of this chapter (the questions and answers) are most appealing to you? Explain your answer.

_____

_____

_____

_____

_____

_____

_____

_____

_____

Take time to go to LoveWhereYouLive.com to browse sermon notes, small group materials, and other resources that will help you in your journey.

_____

_____

_____

_____

_____

_____

_____

_____

_____

_____

www.ingramcontent.com/pod-product-compliance
Lightning Source LLC
Chambersburg PA
CBHW070051100426
42734CB00040B/2980